A GUIDE TO

Adoption &
Orphan Care

A Guide to Adoption and Orphan Care:
Guide Book No. 002
Copyright © 2012 by SBTS Press.

SBTS Press c/o Communications
2825 Lexington Ave.
Louisville, KY 40280

Printed in the United States of America.

ISBN: 978-0615619194

A GUIDE TO

Adoption &
Orphan Care

Russell D. Moore, Editor

GUIDE BOOK NO.

Table of Contents

Biblical
&
Theological
Foundations

Abba Changes Everything

Why every Christian is called to rescue orphans

By Russell D. Moore

The creepiest sound I have ever heard was nothing at all. My wife, Maria, and I stood in the hallway of an orphanage somewhere in the former Soviet Union, on the first of two trips required for our petition to adopt. Orphanage staff led us down a hallway to greet the two one-year-olds we hoped would become our sons. The horror wasn't the squalor and the stench, although we at times stifled the urge to vomit and weep. The horror was the quiet of it all. The place was more silent than a funeral home by night.

I stopped and pulled on Maria's elbow. "Why is it so quiet? The place is filled with babies." Both of us compared the stillness with the buzz and punctuated squeals that came from our church nursery back home. Here, if we listened carefully enough, we could hear babies rocking themselves back and forth, the crib slats gently bumping against the walls. These children did not cry, because infants eventually learn to stop crying if no one ever responds to their calls for food, for comfort, for love. No one ever responded to these children. So they stopped.

The silence continued as we entered the boys' room. Little Sergei (now Timothy) smiled at us, dancing up and down while holding the side of his crib. Little Maxim (now Benjamin) stood straight at attention, regal and czar-like. But neither boy made a sound. We read them books filled with words they couldn't understand, about saying goodnight to the moon and cows jumping over the same. But there were no cries, no squeals, no groans. Every day we left at the appointed time in the same way we entered: in silence.

On the last day of the trip, Maria and I arrived at the moment we had dreaded since the minute we received our adoption referral.

I was struck, maybe for the first time, by the force of the *Abba* cry passages in the New Testament, ones I had memorized in Vacation Bible School.

We had to tell the boys goodbye, as by law we had to return to the United States and wait for the legal paperwork to be completed before returning to pick them up for good. After hugging and kissing them, we walked out into the quiet hallway as Maria shook with tears.

And that's when we heard the scream.

Little Maxim fell back in his crib and let out a guttural yell. It seemed he knew, maybe for the first time, that he would be heard. On some primal level, he knew he had a father and mother now. I will never forget how the hairs on my arms stood up as I heard the yell. I was struck, maybe for the first time, by the force of the *Abba* cry passages in the New Testament, ones I had memorized in Vacation Bible School. And I was surprised by how little I had gotten it until now.

Gospel and mission

When someone learns that I'm going to speak at their church about adoption, typically the first question is, "So will you be talking about the doctrine of adoption or, you know, real adoption?" That's a hard question, because I cannot address one without addressing the other. We cannot master one aspect and then move to the other, from the vertical aspect of adoption to the horizontal aspect, or vice versa.

Without the missional aspect, the doctrine of adoption too easily becomes mere metaphor, just another way to say "saved."

Families, the Bible tells us, reflect something eternally true about God. It is God's fatherhood after which every family in heaven and on earth is named (Eph 3:14-15). We know what human parenting should look like based on our Father's behavior toward us. The reverse is also true. We see something of God's fatherhood in our relationship with our human fathers. Jesus tells us that our fathers' provision and discipline show us God's active love toward us (Matt 7:9-11; Heb 12:5-17).

The same principle is at work in adoption. Adoption is, on one hand, gospel. Our identity and inheritance are grounded in our adoption in Christ. Adoption is also mission. In this, our adoption spurs us to join Christ in advocating for the poor, the marginalized, the abandoned and the fatherless. Without the theological aspect, the growing Christian emphasis on orphan care too often seems like one more cause-wristband for compassionate conservative evangelicals to wear until the trend dies down. Without the missional aspect, the doctrine of adoption too easily becomes mere metaphor, just another way to say "saved."

No natural-born children of God

Little Maxim's scream changed everything – more, I think, than did the judge's verdict and the notarized paperwork. It was the moment, in his recognizing that he would be heard, that he went from being an orphan to being a son. It was also the moment I became a father in fact, if not in law. We both recognized that something was wrong, because suddenly, life as it had been seemed terribly disordered.

Up to that time, I had read the *Abba* cry passages in Romans and Galatians the same way I had heard them preached: as a gurgle of familiarity, the spiritual equivalent of an infant cooing "Papa" or "Daddy." Relational intimacy is surely present in the texts – hence Paul's choice of such a personal word as "*Abba*" – but this definitely isn't sentimental. After all, Scripture tells us that Jesus' Spirit lets our hearts cry "Abba, Father!" (Gal 4:6). Jesus cries "Abba, Father" as he screams "with loud cries and tears" for deliverance in the Garden of Gethsemane (Heb 5:7; Mark 14:36). Similarly, the doctrine of adoption shows us that we "groan" with the creation itself "as we wait eagerly for adoption as sons, the redemption of our bodies" (Rom 8:23). It is the scream of the crucified.

The gospel of adoption challenges us, first of all, to recognize ourselves as spiritual orphans. The gospel compels us to see our fallen universe – and our own egocentric kingdoms therein – as not the way it's supposed to be.

With our evangelistic emphasis on the sinner's prayer, evangelicals ought to recognize this more than we often do. "Everyone who calls on the name of the Lord will be saved" (Rom 10:13), we rightly insist. But we rarely feel how desperate – and how liberating – the call is. We assume it's a cry only at the beginning of the Christian walk, not through the ongoing work of the Spirit. We grow complacent in the present age, too comfortable to cry out for a Father we can sense only by faith.

The *Abba* cry of our adoption defines who we are and to what family we belong. That's why Scripture's witness to the doctrine of adoption has everything to do with church

Scripture's witness to the doctrine of adoption has everything to do with church unity, away from the divisions of Jew and Gentile, slave and free, male and female, rich and poor (Gal 3:28).

unity, away from the divisions of Jew and Gentile, slave and free, male and female, rich and poor (Gal 3:28). None of us are natural-born children of God, entitled to all this grace, all this glory. It's not just the Gentiles – with their uncircumcised penises and pig-flesh-eating mouths – who were adopted into this family. The Jewish Christians, too, received adoption (Rom 9:4). Yes, Abraham was the father of the Israelites, but he was an Iraqi Gentile before he joined the household of God. We Christians receive newcomers because, in Christ, we have been received. Our identity and our inheritance are found in Christ, or they are not found at all.

I was at first reluctant to adopt, because I assumed an adopted child would always be more distant than a child "of my own." I was wrong. And I should have

known better. After all, there are no "adopted children" of God, as an ongoing category. Adoption tells us how we came into the family of God. And once we are here, no distinction is drawn between those at the dinner table. Love based on the preservation and protection of genetic material makes sense in a Darwinian – not a Christian – view of reality.

Thus, the adoption and orphan care movement teaches us something revolutionary about the *evangel*. ᴅᴐ

A Picture of Adoption

Adoption and orphan care in Scripture and
Christian thought

By Timothy Paul Jones

Consider for a moment some of the most familiar stories in our culture. Luke Skywalker in a galaxy far far away and Batman and Robin in Gotham City; Harry Potter at Hogwarts and many of the inhabitants of Charles Xavier's School for Gifted Youngsters; Anne of Green Gables and Dorothy Gale of Kansas; Jane Eyre at Gateshead and Heathcliff in *Wuthering Heights*. All of them are orphans, many of them living as wards of an aunt and uncle. When you look at heroes or central characters in movies and novels, there's a far higher proportion of orphans than in the population as a whole.

So why does the orphan show up so often?

I suspect one reason is that, long before external conflict leads to the climax of the story, the fictional orphan has already endured deep inner turmoil and conflict. Writers are able to create a story where a character has already endured loneliness and loss.

Beyond that, though fallen humanity demands the right to deny it, we identify deep down with orphan characters because we see in them a mirror of ourselves. We are orphans, separated from the heavenly Father. Though these films and fictional texts make no direct reference to the gospel, they needle at our need for the gospel because something deep within us recognizes that we are orphans too.

The Pinocchio syndrome

There's one more fictional character to consider as well. He's not exactly an orphan but he has much to do with adoption. This character is Pinocchio.

The tale of Pinocchio concerns a wooden puppet who longs to be a real boy. In Walt Disney's retelling, Pinocchio serves as Geppetto's substitute for a child – but he's not quite the carver's own real son. (The pre-Disney version of the tale is far stranger and not nearly so sentimental. Geppetto creates Pinocchio because he was tricked into taking an enchanted bit of wood; the puppet murders the cricket; and, the blue fairy sends a poodle to rescue Pinocchio.) Unfortunately, this idea of something not quite real that can be substituted for a real child isn't limited to Walt Disney films. When talking about adoption, I constantly hear proof of what I call "the Pinocchio syndrome": "Do you know who your daughter's 'real parents' were?" "We're interested in adoption but we want to have

> Though fallen humanity demands the right to deny it, we identify deep down with orphan characters because we see in them a mirror of ourselves.

our 'own children' first." "Those three are their 'real kids' then they adopted the others later."

So if birthparents are "real parents" what are adoptive parents? Artificial parents? Substitute moms and dads?

If you want to have your "own children" first, what are adopted children? Somebody else's children?

If children birthed from the bodies of you and your spouse are "real kids," are adopted children unreal? Are they, like Pinocchio, substitutes for the real thing?

The Pinocchio syndrome is just as apparent, though a bit more insidious, when someone says, "I don't know that I could love an adopted child the same way I would love my own child" or "I couldn't accept a child from another race in the same way as my own child." An adopted child is viewed as something less than a real son or daughter.

It doesn't help that the English term "adopt" gets applied everywhere from highways to

While cleaning up hamburger wrappers along the highway and picking up your next pet at the animal shelter are certainly to be commended, those deeds are in an entirely different category from adopting a child.

humane societies. Look up "adopt" on the Internet and you'll find far more references to adoption of animals than to children. While cleaning up hamburger wrappers along the highway and picking up your next pet at the animal shelter are certainly to be commended, those deeds are in an entirely different category from adopting a child. Yet I cannot tell you the number of times my sanctification has been tested after I have spoken about adoption when someone begins telling me about their recent adoption of a dog, as if these two processes are somehow the same. Truly, I am sure that someone, somewhere, is thrilled that this animal is finally sleeping through the night – but please don't expect me to be as excited about your Schnauzer as I am about a parentless child who now has a home.

These patterns tell us as much about our perception of the gospel as they do about our perception of adoption. If my daughters are not my "real" daughters because

> An adopted child is not a substitute to satisfy our longing for a real child. Jesus is the sole substitute who is sufficient to satisfy the longings of our souls.

they're adopted, you and I are not quite God's "real" children; you are not quite God's "own" child; Jesus is not quite your "real" brother. If you are not God's real child and if Jesus is not my real brother, you and I are still lost in our sins.

An adopted child is not a substitute to satisfy our longing for a real child. Jesus is the sole substitute who is sufficient to satisfy the longings of our souls. To see an adopted child as a substitute for the better gift of a biological child treats the adopted child as a lesser gift and repudiates the sufficiency of what God has done for us through Jesus. Through the work of Jesus, we are adopted as God's own real children. All this talk about adoption is not simply about how to gain another tax deduction; it has to do with how we perceive and practice the gospel.

Adoption in the Old Testament

As Adam and Eve stood there in the garden, clutching fig leaves that failed to cover nakedness, that was not merely the unveiling of flesh but an inescapable shadow in the soul, God spoke the words to the woman:

> I will surely multiply your pain in childbearing; in pain you shall bring forth

> Adoption is one example of an instance in which a greater good comes from the Fall. The Fall happens and it's a bad thing, but God turns that into a good greater than would have been without the Fall.

children. Your desire shall be for your husband, and he shall rule over you (Gen 3:16).

These words represent the foundations of orphanhood.

Because of the Fall, childbearing becomes not only a source of happiness and hope but also a source of pain. What once would have been only joyful now becomes flecked with sorrow. Parents will long for children and not be able to bear them. Parents will conceive children but lose them. Children will have parents and then lose them. The world that God once pronounced "very good" will become a context for the loss of children and for the making of orphans.

Adoption would never have occurred apart from the Fall, but at the same time adoption expresses something good. Adoption is a prime example of *felix culpa*.

Felix culpa means "fortunate fall" in Latin. In his *Summa Theologica*, Thomas Aquinas speaks of it this way:

> *For God allows evils to happen in order to bring a greater good therefrom; hence it is written: "Where sin abounded, grace did more abound." Hence, too, in the blessing of the Paschal candle, we say: "O happy fault, that merited such and so great a Redeemer!"*

Adoption is one example of an instance in which a greater good comes from the Fall. The Fall happens and it's a bad thing, but God turns that into a good greater than would have been without the Fall. Adoption is a living expression of *felix culpa*.

We have the foundation of orphanhood in the Fall of humanity. But we also see that

God works through adoption for a greater good than possible apart from the Fall. The Torah also shows us the foundations for orphan. The Hebrew word that's translated "orphan" means "alone" and that's one of the primary words for an orphan, for one who is fatherless. Remember that culturally, the father is a protector and guide, not simply an economic relationship. All of those things are bound up together in fatherhood. Apart from a father, the child is truly and authentically alone.

Throughout the Old Testament, God calls for the community of Israel to care for orphans. In the book of Deuteronomy, we see a three-pronged theme of care for the orphan, the widow and the stranger. Israel should make certain to care for these. And then one of the interesting things in the Book of Job is that Job uses his care for orphans to express that he truly is a righteous person. He says, "If I have raised my hand against the fatherless ... then let my shoulder blade fall from my shoulder, and let my arm be broken from its socket." Job also mentions that the wicked ignore the needs of the orphan. Psalm 68 expresses this. It's clear in the Old Testament that the heart of God is for the orphan, and he expects the hearts of his people to reflect his.

The foundations for orphan care and adoption are present in the Torah as well as all through the Old Testament. However, instances of adoption are rare. In fact, we only see three clear occurrences in the Old Testament: Moses in Exodus 2:10; Esther in Esther 2:7, 15; and Genubath (you will now have a great name for one of your children) in 1 Kings 11:20. That's it. And even these aren't quite the type of adoption about which we're talking.

I remember when my family struggled with wanting children; we faced spending $10,000 on fertility treatments. It tore at me. It seemed like, as I looked at Scripture, everyone who cries out for a child gets one. They call out to God and he provides a child in a biological way. It appeared to us that fertility treatments were the only choice open if we wanted what, at that time, I would have called my "own" children. The stories in the Bible ripped at me.

How does adoption seem unthinkable in the Old Testament but become a key metaphor in the New Testament? The answer is Jesus.

Think about Abraham and Sarah, Isaac and Rebekah and Israel and Rachael. And then places in the Pentateuch promise that if a person is righteous, then he or she will have children: Manoah, the father of Samson, and Hannah and her husband, Elkanah. They cry out to God for a child and they receive one.

Be aware of how Scripture itself can discourage those who want children. Of course, we don't use Scripture correctly when we're discouraged about children. But we need to think through this because we come up with questions like, "If, in the Old Testament, God always leads his people to pregnancy, why not us?" How does adoption seem unthinkable in the Old Testament but become a key metaphor in the New Testament?

The answer is Jesus.

Adoption in the New Testament

Jesus revolutionizes how we understand family and children. In Jesus, we see a radical change in the perception of children that results in a radical change in the perception of adoption. In the Old Testament, the barren have children. This is part of God's ongoing promise that he will provide a seed who will crush the serpent's head. Jesus fulfills that promise in the New Testament.

In the Old Testament, the barren conceive in order the bring about in God's time the promise of Genesis 3:15. And then in the New Testament, a virgin conceives and bears a son who is the longed-for answer to Israel's barrenness. Jesus breaks the power of the curse that began in Eden.

Jesus sets an axe to the notion that we are who we are because of our physical, biological pedigree. Look at Matthew 3:9-10:

And do not presume to say to yourselves, "We have Abraham as our father," for I tell you, God is able from these stones to raise up children for Abraham. Even now the axe is laid to the root of the trees. Every tree therefore that does not bear good fruit is cut down and thrown into the fire.

In other words, John the Baptist says, "Do not judge yourselves by your physical pedigree, rather, recognize that your identity is in Jesus Christ." Remember when Jesus says that "my mother, brothers, sisters are those who do the will of my Father in heaven"? This radically changes everything going on in the Old Testament.

The death of Jesus activates our adoption. Yet he didn't stay dead.

When Paul writes to the Romans, he builds on the Roman practice of adoption to illustrate the new realities found in Christ.

Romans were familiar with adoption. In fact, five of the first-century emperors were adopted: Octavian, also known as Augustus; Caesar Tiberius; Caligula also known as Gaius; Claudius; and Nero. Often we don't recognize that when the Book of Romans addresses adoption, the Roman citizens saw it in their politics.

Adoption was a significant transaction in Rome. The culture operated under the principle, *patria potestas*, which means that the father was sovereign over his children. The child had no rights. Adoption, then, was enacted through death. By the death of the father, his name and inheritance were conveyed to the son. This, of course, is immensely important for us theologically. To receive an inheritance, the child must bear his father's name. It's the same for us.

The death of Jesus activates our adoption. Yet he didn't stay dead. And by taking his name, we receive Jesus' inheritance with him. We must understand this when we look at Romans. In particular, think about Romans 8:14-17. Paul writes:

For all who are led by the Spirit of God are sons of God. For you did not receive the spirit of slavery to fall back into fear, but you have received the Spirit of adoption as sons, by whom we cry, "Abba! Father!" The Spirit himself bears witness with our spirit that we are children of God, and if children, then heirs – heirs of God and fellow heirs with Christ, provided we suffer

Paul then reminds both Jews and Gentiles that they began as orphans. They were both lost, both alienated from the Father.

with him in order that we may also be glorified with him.

The Holy Spirit co-testifies with our spirit that we are co-heirs. We co-suffer. We will be co-glorified. That's adoption.

When Paul writes this, Jews in the Roman church basically say that they are the children of God by flesh and the Gentiles are adopted into the family. In essence the Jews suggest that they are God's Plan A and Gentiles are God's Plan B. Now the Gentiles say back, "Your people rejected God as father. You rejected him and then God chose to adopt us."

Paul then reminds both groups that they began as orphans. They were both lost, both alienated from the Father. In chapter one, look at what the Gentiles did with the knowledge that God gave them. They turned it into perversity and idolatry. At this time, all the Jews in the church cheer, "Go, Paul!" But he turns to the Jews in chapter two. He condemns their use of the law that God gave them. Their righteousness, what they did with the law, didn't avail anything. Then, in chapter three, Paul makes

Paul does not let us escape, however, that this relationship was birthed in the suffering of Jesus. This adoption is centered in the cross of Christ and thus we inherit the Father's blessing.

clear that no one, neither Jew nor Gentile, is righteous – no not one.

Paul pursues this argument to let the church know that the adoption of Jews and Gentiles is not God's Plan B. Adoption is God's Plan A. From the beginning, God planned redemption, for all people, through adoption. None of us deserve to be God's sons. For all of us, God makes us his sons by adoption through his Spirit. Paul says that those of you who are adopted, are so by God's choice. You cry out to him "Abba, Father" in order to communicate simultaneously sovereignty and intimacy.

I remember the first time that Hannah came to visit with us. We had already chosen her, and everything had been approved for the adoption at that time. The social worker told us, "Whatever you do, don't let her call you 'daddy' or 'father,' because you could change your mind and you don't want to devastate her." And then when Hannah showed up, she immediately asked, "Well, what do I call you?" And I said, "You can call me 'Daddy.' That's who I am to you and it doesn't depend on you – I'm your father and that's the way it is."

Any time a Jewish individual reads Romans 8, they think about Abraham. I think specifically about Genesis 17:7, where God promises "to be God to [Abraham] and to [his] offspring after [him]." God fulfills this promise in Jesus.

Paul does not let us escape, however, that this relationship was birthed in the suffering of Jesus. This adoption is centered in the cross of Christ and just as we inherit the Father's blessing with Christ, we too will suffer with him. We co-inherit with him that we may be co-glorified with him.

Those of you who are thinking

about adoption, there is a very strong possibility that you are going to suffer in the process. But all of our suffering is co-suffering with Jesus. The New Testament presents Jesus as both the redemption and the redeemer of his people.

Adoption in church history

The early church understood the implications of Jesus as redeemed and the redeemer. From a relatively early time, Christians cared for and even adopted abandoned children. In fact, by the time of the Council of Arles (A.D. 314), the church outlined the proper way to adopt. So before the council, adoption must have been commonplace.

Sometime in the A.D. 200s, The Didascalia says that "if any are unwilling to adopt the orphan because they would rather please man, or if they are by reason of their wealth ashamed to have an orphan, may strangers devour their land before their eyes." Basically, he says that if people fear the social effects of orphan care, then may their lands be fruitless and dissolve. People in this time period seemed to understand clearly that adoption is an implication of the gospel.

We ought to reflect the gospel to the point where the world sees clearly that Christians desire and love any child of any color, any background. Any young woman who walks into a Planned Parenthood clinic, knows well that a host of people would love her child and love the mother – recognizing that she is an orphan. I believe that this happened in the early church.

We should ask, "What about this child? What could this child become?" There can be no worse pedigree than the one from which you and I came: we are children of the devil. It doesn't get worse than that. We should look at a child and consider him or her that way.

I remember when we adopted Hannah, she came with a file. A lot of things happened in foster care that was messed up, some of which she perpetrated, others of which had been perpetrated. My wife and I had to sign disclaimers stating that we won't sue the agency

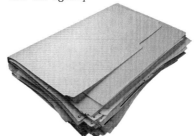

because the child has this or that. "What are we getting ourselves into with this box of papers," we thought. Then it struck me. What does my stack of papers look like, if God were to put me on paper? Yet God chose to love, to adopt, and to make me – and you – co-heirs with him.

Adoption in Christian theology

Think about adoption in terms of creation, fall, redemption and consummation.

IN LIGHT OF CREATION, every child is a gift. It doesn't matter who their parents are or who their parents used to be or what they've done, every child is a gift.

IN LIGHT OF THE FALL, however, every child is a sinner. Only one child is sufficient to satisfy your soul, and he is Jesus Christ. Something that often happens in adoptive couples is the idea that if only they got a child, then everything would be okay. They place expectations on a child that he or she can never fulfill. The child becomes a Messiah. I remember painfully learning to say, "God, if we ever get a child or not, I will still be satisfied in you." That's hard to say. Sometimes in fact – let's just be honest – a child ends up bringing more stress and pain

If I stand beside my child in eternity, I will not stand beside her as her father; she will not stand beside me as my daughter. In eternity, we will be brother and sister.

into your life than you had before you were parents.

Decide before adopting that whether a child ever comes or not, you will find your satisfaction and identity in God. If not, you might end up torn into pieces in your own relationship with your spouse and in your relationship with your child, because you thought the child could provide something he or she simply can't.

IN LIGHT OF REDEMPTION, every child needs a savior. Part of our adoption process is recognizing that adoption is an evangelistic effort. The world around us does not want to hear that. If you look at the popular-level articles about the adoption movement, many sources give a harsh critique. The world wants to convert children to their god, just as we want to convert children to ours.

We want to place children in a context where we can be a means of grace in his or her life. Children in households of believers are more likely to come to faith. And God, in some way, uses this as a means by which he brings people to faith in him. In adoption, we join in God's mission of seeking to bring people to Jesus Christ.

IN LIGHT OF CONSUMMATION, every child is forever. Don't forget that. Your family is not forever, but children are and you are. We raise children and seek children thinking about forever. If I stand beside my child in eternity, I will not stand beside her as her father; she will not stand beside me as my daughter. In eternity, we will be brother and sister. Every child is forever. As in every area of eschatology, we must practice now what we expect to do in eternity. And in eternity, we will worship as a community of believers. So, according to Romans, we wait eagerly for our adoption as sons, the redemption of our bodies. We wait for that time when God will reveal the ways in which we are his children. And here and now, we wait eagerly for this future by pursuing a lifestyle of adoption now.

Conclusion

What are you going to do here and now to live a lifestyle of adoption? For some, that means pursuing adoption. For others, that means helping a family in the midst of adoption, maybe financially, maybe just loving and caring for them. And for some, that means that there are kids in your church whose parents have disengaged from them and you've become a "family in faith" for them. You don't adopt them legally – not illegally either – you relationally pour yourself into them. That's part of a lifestyle of adoption. We receive from others and we model in the lives of others what it means to love the orphan, to love the widow, to care for those who are in an orphan category. How will you anticipate the adoption God has already guaranteed? It's already real, it's already true, but he will reveal the full glory of our adoption at the end of time. ॐ

Our Paper Pregnancy

God, the gospel and the global cause of Christ

By David A. Gundersen

They call it a "paper pregnancy." It's the period of time between the conception and finalization of your adoption. There's no positive pregnancy test; no hormonal upheaval; no morning sickness; no amazing ultrasounds; no growing belly; no random food cravings; no little feet-kicks coming from the womb; no agonizing labor pains or delivery. Yet each of these finds its reflection in the paper pregnancy.

Our first was 19 months long.

We decided to adopt in December 2005, and I picked up my wife and our 18-month-old Ugandan son at the airport on July 13, 2007. Our positive pregnancy test was the U.S. government's acceptance of our application. Our hormonal turmoil was the onslaught of emotions that flow from the ups-and-downs of pioneer adoptions in African countries. The morning sickness came in frustrations of all kinds, from paperwork pains to cross-governmental headaches to the dizziness and nausea caused by the roller-coaster of international bureaucracy. The surreal ultrasound came in the first picture we ever received of the baby boy with whom we were "matched up" and the periodic arrival of pictures during the months functioned as many kicks and somersaults in the womb, reminding us that our son was real, alive and growing. As the process lengthened, the anticipation bulged and, at the end of it all, came the agonizing labor pains of my wife's second trip to Uganda and her final week in the capital city – which she will tell you was the most hectic and hair-raising week of her life.

Why go through this? The same question that women throughout

> We ourselves have experienced the grace of adoption, and on a much grander scale. We were slaves of sin, but are now children of God (Rom 8:15). God was our judge, but now he is our Father (John 1:12).

the centuries have asked in the pains of delivery can be asked of those who chose to walk through a predictably intense adoption: "Why?"

It wasn't because we wanted a child and couldn't have one on our own. We were a young couple, and we actually just wanted to adopt first. Scripture doesn't have a "plan B" view of adoption.

We've never discovered a verse presenting adoption simply as a second-rate way to grow a family. We're overjoyed at friends who decide to adopt because they can't have biological children, and their children are no less blessed because adoption wasn't their parents' initial choice. But family-building is not the main motivation for helping the fatherless.

Rather, the highest and best motivation for adopting is the gospel of Jesus Christ. The spiritual impulse to adopt runs far deeper than cute international babies, cross-cultural experiences and family growth. The impulse to adopt echoes from the very heartbeat of the gospel.

We ourselves have experienced the grace of adoption, and on a much grander scale. We were slaves of sin, but are now children of God (Rom 8:15). God was our judge, but now he is our Father (John 1:12). We faced a foreboding future in hell, but now we anticipate an abundant inheritance in heaven (Rom 8:16-17). God is the Father of the fatherless (Ps 68:5), and he has made himself that for us through Jesus Christ. Adoption is in our blood. Adoption is in God's blood.

The rights of sonship

Adoption has been called the "crown jewel of redemption," because even justification and reconciliation do not have to include adoption. God could have rescued us from sin and death without becoming our Father. It is possible to have reconciliation without sonship, to have justification without adoption. We could have been predestined, foreknown, called, justified, sanctified and glorified without being adopted, because

a declaration of righteousness is not the same as a declaration of sonship. Yet those of us who are in Christ are far more than former debtors and forgiven criminals. We are God's children.

At 11:36 a.m., Friday, Nov. 16, 2007, at Children's Court in Monterrey Park, Calif., Judge John L. Henning declared that Judah David Mukisa Gundersen is the

legal son of Cynthia and David Gundersen, with all the rights and privileges of a natural-born child, including inheritance. We swore under oath that we would treat him as such, and the judge signed the court order to that effect. Although this was the first time we had walked through this process, these weren't strange words to us. For years we've read them in the Bible. These words are our story.

This is why Jesus' earliest followers wrote things like this in their letters: "Pure and undefiled religion in the sight of our God and Father is this: to visit orphans and widows in their distress, and to keep oneself unstained by the world" (Jas 1:27). This call to help the helpless resounds in the heart of all who have been "visited" by God in Christ and who have been helped in their "distress."

The needs of orphans worldwide are incalculable. Their "distress" is severe. And we have the gospel, a family and a home (in that order). With all of this in mind, the thought of our not helping orphans is unthinkable. We adopt because he first adopted us (1 John 4:19).

With international adoption, there's another element at play. God loves diversity, and we love diversity with him. Unity in the midst of diversity is beautiful because it displays the singular glory of the one who binds the diversity together. Jesus Christ is praised in the Book of Revelation because, as the four living creatures and the 24

God loves diversity, and we love diversity with him. Unity in the midst of diversity is beautiful because it displays the singular glory of the one who binds the diversity together.

This is why, at the end of it all, we want to bring the children of the nations into our family – not so that they can grow up and live the American dream, but so that by God's grace they can grow up and walk the narrow road.

elders cry out, "You were slain, and purchased for God with your blood men from every tribe and tongue and people and nation" (Rev 5:9). God's family is colorful, because God is creative and because the bond of Christ is strong. This is magnificent to us, and for as long as I can remember I've wanted our family to mirror this every-tribe-tongue-people-nation diversity. The loveliest family in all the universe is God's, and its loveliness is well worth reflecting.

The global cause of Christ

Finally, a word about adoption and the global cause of Christ. Missions means spreading the name of Jesus Christ to every nook and cranny of every people group on the planet by crossing cultures and languages and geographical boundaries to reach them – whether they be urban socialites or desert nomads or tribal villagers. International adoption means spreading the name of Jesus Christ into the hearts and lives of every people group on the planet by crossing

cultures and languages and ethnic barriers to bring the smallest and neediest of the world's population into our homes, making them part of our families and investing the gospel into their lives from the backyard to the dinner table to the bedside. Adoption and the global Christian mission are inseparable.

This is why, at the end of it all, we want to bring the children of the nations into our family – not so that they can grow up and live the American dream, but so that by God's grace they can grow up and walk the narrow road. Running water, medical care and a sound education are precious and valuable things. But seeing the glory of Christ, hearing the good news of salvation, finding reconciliation with God and walking in a manner worthy of the incarnate Savior of the world is infinitely more precious.

And so we seek to adopt – as those who have been freely adopted ourselves into a beautifully diverse family unified in the death, burial and resurrected reign of Jesus Christ; as those who have been called to the outreaching of global missions and the in-bringing of Christian adoption; and as those whose hearts long not for the security and comfort of the American dream but for radical

> And so we seek to adopt – as those who have been freely adopted ourselves.

lives of incarnational love.

Every day, I see all of this and more in the bright eyes and brilliant smile and childlike faith of my children. I see the grace of God. I see the gospel of Christ. I see the diversity of the church. And I see the call of the Christian mission. And perhaps most of all, I see that it is no small thing to be a child, and no small thing to have a father.

"For you did not receive the spirit of slavery to fall back into fear, but you have received the Spirit of adoption as sons, by whom we cry out, 'Abba! Father!' The Spirit himself bears witness with our spirit that we are children of God, and if children, then heirs – heirs of God and fellow heirs with Christ, provided we suffer with him in order that we may also be glorified with him" (Rom 8:15-17). ✎

For Parents

Don't You Already Have Kids?

Adding to your existing family through adoption

By Randy Stinson

"I can hardly breathe," I told my wife. And I meant it. We were in an old elevator headed to the third floor of a battered women's shelter in downtown Taipei City, Taiwan just seconds before meeting our two new daughters. They were five-and-a-half and three-and-a-half years old respectively, and were just as nervous as we were. The social workers blandly announced to the girls, "Here's your mama, and here's your papa." They handed us a bag of clothes that didn't fit and sent us on our way. No fanfare. No celebration. No instructions.

It was one of the greatest days of our lives. It was also the culmination of years of conviction, hard work, bureaucracy, patience (impatience) and prayer. The most common question we heard through the whole process was, "Don't you already have kids?"

What those people meant was, "Why would you adopt when you can obviously have kids biologically?" We had three biological children but it never crossed our minds that we should not add to our family through the gift of adoption. Here are the factors that drove our decision to adopt:

WE ARE COMMITTED TO LIFE.
For our entire marriage we have supported many pro-life causes. But we always felt that if we were going to encourage unwed girls to give birth to their babies, then Christians should be in line, ready to adopt those children given up. It was our way of putting our "money where our mouths were."

WE ARE COMMITTED TO THE HELPLESS AND DISADVANTAGED.
James (1:27) makes clear that one of the evidences of our faith is how we

We are committed to gospel-centeredness. The doctrine of adoption is at the heart of the gospel. We are born outside of Christ, but through Christ we receive "the Spirit of adoption as sons, by whom we cry 'Abba! Father!'" (Rom 8:15).

respond to the "affliction" of widows and orphans. Taking care of these two groups is time consuming, messy and sacrificial. But it's a central part of the Christian life. We wanted to make sure that our family was heavily invested in this important admonition.

WE ARE COMMITTED TO BIBLICAL MANHOOD.

God calls men to lead, provide and protect (Gen 1-2; Eph 5:22-33; 1 Kings 2:1-9; 1 Pet 3:1-7; Col 3:18-25). This is a fundamental teaching in the Bible and it does not merely pertain to the four walls of the home. Men should look for those who need protection and provision. There are fatherless children all across the world. Every year I meet women burdened for adoption but their husbands won't budge. It's usually something about retirement, college costs or finally being able to afford that boat they always wanted. In our home, the men lead and sacrificially give of themselves for the good of others.

WE ARE COMMITTED TO GOSPEL-CENTEREDNESS.

The doctrine of adoption is at the heart of the gospel. We are born outside of Christ, but through Christ we receive "the Spirit of adoption as sons, by whom we cry 'Abba! Father!'" (Rom 8:15). Physical adoption is a daily, living picture of this spiritual reality. It is a constant reminder to our family and others of the grace and mercy of God and his love for the lost and care for the fatherless.

WE ARE COMMITTED TO THE NATIONS.

God doesn't call everyone to international adoption, but the

Physical adoption is a daily, living picture of this spiritual reality. It is a constant reminder to our family and others of the grace and mercy of God and his love for the lost and care for the fatherless.

result is a reminder of God's love for every "nation and tribe and language and people" (Rev 14:6). Every week the Lord adds people to his church and tells you and me to love them. They may not look like we do, smell like we do, have the same socio-economic background as we do or talk like we do. But that's the beauty of the gospel. Twice we have brought into our home children from another country and told our other kids, "They don't talk like you or look like you, but here's another one; love them." It has been one of the biggest blessings in the whole process for us and has dramatically shaped our view of the whole world.

Maybe the next big decision in your life will involve a vacation house or a boat or a car that you don't need. Maybe it will involve trying to stock away more money for that early retirement for which you're hoping. It might even involve

That's the beauty of the gospel. Twice we have brought into our home children from another country and told our other kids, "They don't talk like you or look like you, but here's another one; love them."

contributing to a monument or building with your name on it. Or, just maybe, it will involve an old elevator in another country with your mind in a whirl, your heart racing, adrenaline rushing and your lungs struggling inexplicably for their next breath. And in making that decision, it might not even cross your mind that you already have kids. ॐ১

Adoption Road Map
Navigating the often winding road of adoption

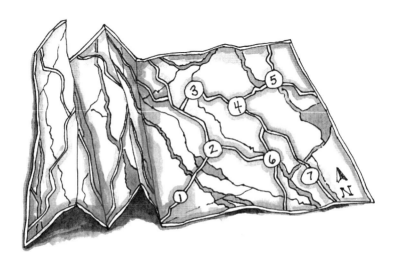

By Dan Dumas

Make your plans in pencil. This is good advice for your career, for your marriage and, yes, for your adoption. When my wife, Jane, and I adopted our second son, our inked-in plans blew up in our faces. There we were, expanding our family, trying to promote the gospel through adoption. And everything went wrong.

A few years ago, a pastor-friend of mine in lower Alabama called me. The 18-year-old granddaughter of a woman in his church was pregnant. The youthful girl and her boyfriend – with whom she already had one child – didn't think they could handle another baby. So our friends asked if we might be interested in bringing this child into our home. Jane and I said without hesitation, "Absolutely."

Like our previous adoption, this one would be a private adoption – which is our preferred method – so we went down to Alabama and met with the mother and father. When we left, everything seemed set and almost too simple. However, dealing with the couple turned out to be a precarious venture.

A month later, we received another call: "The doctor will induce the mother at 9 a.m." Crazy, the baby would arrive early the next morning. My wife called and told me around 5 p.m. We hadn't packed a thing. We didn't have a place to stay in Alabama. We were nine hours away. But we jumped in the car and started driving like crazy (viewing the speed limit more as a suggestion).

About nine hours later, having missed the birth by about 45 minutes, we were met by a social worker who appeared to have a concerned look on her face. She announced the baby was born; mom was doing just fine. But

The social worker announced, "We recommend you turn around and go home. The state will take the child from here." But my resolved wife, the dutiful mom, said, "No. We're all in."

the baby boy for whom we had hoped and prayed was addicted to cocaine.

He shook. He quivered all over as his little body went through withdrawal. They said he was going to be a medical mess. The social worker announced, "We recommend you turn around and go home. The state will take the child from here." But my resolved wife, the dutiful mom, said, "No. We're all in." Turning back now was not an option and we sensed this was a part of God's sovereign

New Testament scholar D. A. Carson often refers to the "peculiar providence of God." We experienced this firsthand as we were preparing the court documents, staying out of the public eye and praying like crazy.

plan. And, credit only to God's merciful hands, the little guy ended up just fine.

Now according to Alabama state law, the birth mother had 72 hours in which she could decide not to give up her child and reverse her consent to adopt. When we talked with the birth mom on Friday and departed the hospital going our separate ways, everything was great. Saturday, she called to ask about him. Sunday arrived; we could see our adoption just over the horizon. Then Monday morning, sure enough, our attorney called us with a shocking request.

Our new child had to return to the courts immediately. We had decided theologically, if the birth mother wanted the baby then we needed to step out of the picture. But there was a twist that I had not considered. At the encouragement of our lawyer, who informed us that because of the cocaine-addiction the baby would go to social services, we decided to fight for custody.

The child, we planned to call him "Elijah," had to be turned over before the afternoon, or the state would issue kidnapping charges against Jane and me. What I didn't understand then was that birth parents have rights within the context of an adoption process. Our lawyer said we would need to demonstrate to the court that the mother's character, based on her cocaine use, was such that she didn't make a fitting parent. Even if we did convince the courts, we would still need to receive temporary custody only to fight for adoption later. And what's more, that process would most likely be costly, with only a 50 percent chance of winning since the courts typically side with birth parents.

What in the world! None of this was supposed to happen. This didn't follow our inked-in outline for adoption. So the plot thickened. Furthermore, I needed to return this precious child or face kidnapping charges. I was a church planter and an executive at Southern Seminary; I am supposed to be responsible and live an exemplary life. Kidnapping a child doesn't typically look great on a pastoral resumé.

New Testament scholar D.A. Carson often refers to the "peculiar providence of God." We experienced this firsthand as we were preparing the court documents, staying out of the public eye and praying like crazy. But when everything was fastidiously prepared, we contacted the birth mother to inform her of our plans. But before we could speak, she had reconsidered, a reversal of her reversal, and now decided that the

I am supposed to be responsible. Kidnapping a child doesn't typically look great on a pastoral resumé.

Dumas family could provide her baby with the better home. This cocaine-born little baby would, after all, become Elijah Seth Dumas. Amidst our relief and elation, there would be yet another 72-hour cooling off period.

Finally, after a painful and confusing two weeks, Elijah was ours.

With two adoptions now complete, we have discovered that adoption is complex. It's messy. It certainly requires a strong spiritual constitution. Through the entire processes, I constantly recalled the words of Abraham Kuyper when he said, "There's not a square inch in the whole dominion of human existence over which Christ, who is sovereign over all, does not cry 'Mine!'" That includes my family. My marriage. My adoption process.

Never forget and always rehearse

When you adventure through a process like the one my wife and I did – all adoptions are adventures and each presents its own set of unique circumstances and challenges – you learn a lot about yourself and about your marriage. Like anything else, you can either learn these lessons by personal experience or from secondary experience. From my adoption adventures, I've learned 12 axiomatic and theological-informed principles that I believe will help you navigate the daunting and sometimes messy journey of adoption.

 1.

We live in a fallen world.

Messy. Complicated. Depraved. We are in a Genesis 3 world. From the outset you have to realize that adoption doesn't fit in a neat little box. You might be tempted to think, because adoption is popular and so gospel focused, that it would be all tidied up, pretty, and delivered with tissue paper and fancy packaging. It's not. But it's nothing to fear. God's on your side. He is looking out for what is best and particularly he's working things out for his glory.

2.

Resist making adoption an idol.

Adopting can offer a quick trip down the path of idolatry. Don't go there. The Lord will work out the particulars, trust me. Adoption is part of the gospel; God has a heart for the orphans – James 1:27. If anyone cares about your adoption process, it's your heavenly Father who adopted you – Romans 8. You must guard your heart against idolatry and trust God with the process.

3.

Patience is king.

Cooler heads prevail. I'm a guy who likes structure – no seriously, I like things buttoned up. As a way of ministry, I make disorderly things orderly. That's my specialty. The adopting process messes with my world because it's not nice and clean. However, it is good for the soul. It

sanctifies. I confess, impatience is a besetting flaw in my character. The process of adopting our two sons pushed every impatient button in my body. Today I confess that is a good thing. Good for my character. Maybe more importantly, good for my future, since, for some reason, raising children and impatience are awe-inspiring bedfellows. Remember, Adoption is not for the faint of heart.

4

Display the gospel to everyone involved.

Be a salt-and-light Christian. When you engage in adoption, instantly you have an option to share the gospel, which in a peculiar way will require of you to be seasoned, graceful and kind. Jesus said to be "wise as a serpent and gentle as a dove." Since it is an unnatural process (a mom and dad giving up their child) everyone involved is typically on edge. Picture the wedding day of a new bride times 10. Your sphere of influence will be massive – caseworkers, the agency, the home study, the birth parents and future grandparents and then add friends visiting the birth mother and family in the hospital. Most important, we must display the gospel in all of its self-denying grandeur. Remember this will require of you to die to yourself daily.

5

Pillow your head on God's sovereignty.

The old English theologian and preacher Charles Haddon Spurgeon used to say, "Pillow your head on the sovereignty of God." It seems Spurgeon understood Proverbs 16:1-4,

The plans of the heart belong to man, but the answer of the tongue is from the Lord. All the ways of a man are pure in his own eyes, but the Lord weighs the spirit. Commit your work to the Lord, and your plans will be established. The Lord has made everything for its purpose, even the wicked for the day of trouble.

We have to confess that my adoption plans and your adoption plans are in God's hands. He directs them. And the results will accord with his will. In spite of the messiness God's will prevails.

6. Get your theology in order.

Pre-determine not to get frustrated when the drama comes. Stability and rock solid faith will be required. Adopting is not for the faint of heart. You must strive to give "a soft answer because a soft answer turns away wrath" (Prov 15:1). Refuse to make your children – even your potential children – an idol. Be patient. Persevere. Although it sounds simplistic, trust God through the entire process. And to the fathers, we must lead throughout the process so that we bring theology to bear on the home and speak into the adoption process. Our wives crave and desire our leadership, especially in uncharted waters. Remember, genuine theology walks, not just talks.

Assess your family's constitution.

Early on, you must have specific conversations addressing important questions about your family's wherewithal to adopt. How far are you willing to go medically? What if your child is born addicted to cocaine? What if the child is handicapped? Quadriplegic? Are you willing to adopt a special needs-child? A bi-racial baby? How far you are willing to go needs to be predetermined so that at the moment of decision, you know where to stand. You need to evaluate your will, the will of your spouse, and the will of your other children.

Research your options.

There are a ton of options available to you. Each one has its strengths and weaknesses. You can pursue private adoption, foster care adoption, domestic adoption, international adoption or, in some cases, snowflake or embryo adoption. None are easy and all will require tremendous grace. Remember that all adoptions can be messy, so pursue the door God opens – the ideal on paper doesn't always materialize.

Own the whole process.

If you're thinking about adoption or you're engaged in it currently, get your affairs in order. If you think buying a home has a lot of paperwork, just wait until you see the adoption process. As a general admonition, I should be able to go in your home and you take me to your single location and system where you have all your family documents, whether it's in a safe or some kind of a notebook. All your personal affairs need to be in an easily accessible location and system, including insurance information, passport information, family history and adoption paperwork.

10. *Pray like crazy.*

You must be a family of prayer. Dependence upon Christ's aid is crucial throughout the process. Prayer serves as a means of trusting the sovereignty of God. Robust theology drives us to prayer. When it comes to your adoption, the spiritual warfare will be intense; you don't want to fight by mere physical means. You must be in prayer. Remember, godly men and leaders lead from their knees.

11. Go public with your intentions.

It's what I call "making noise." Private adoptions worked well for our family because I told everyone we'd take any baby and were eager to adopt. Tell everyone at your church that you're interested in adopting. Inevitably, someone will know of

someone who gets coupled with the sovereignty of God, and connect you with people – be a networker. Take advantage of social media to let people know you want to adopt. You'll be surprised at how the Lord brings you a child.

12. Pursue good coaching.

One last time, adoption doesn't fit in a neat little box. Proverbs 18:1 says that he who seeks his own way is a fool. You need a group of people around you who can give you advice and coaching. Seek out couples in your church that have adopted. They can share their experience with you and offer encouragement in the process. Also, dig deep into the growing number of resources available concerning adoption. Read everything you can get your hands on. ⌾⌾

Should We Sterilize Ourselves?

A false dichotomy in a right-minded question

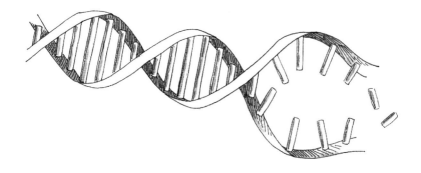

By Russell D. Moore

Dr. Moore,
My wife and I really resonate with your emphasis on orphan care and adoption, caring for widows and the fatherless. We believe God is calling us to minister to orphans through adoption and foster care. We're a young couple, married about three years. We have no children at this time, both finishing up college and graduate school.

Here's our question: We know there are so many children in the world (and in our community) who need parents. We would like to help the maximum number of kids we can. We are contemplating not having children biologically at all, proceeding either by contraception or a vasectomy for me.

We think this is a good idea, and honoring to the Lord. Some of our Christian friends don't think we're making the right decision. What do you think?

Dear Friend,

The people of God, it seems to me, are perpetually pulled toward replacing a "both/and" ethic with an "either/or." That's what I think might be happening here.

Don't get me wrong. The Scripture is often "either/or." It is either God or Baal, either Jesus or Mammon, either Spirit or carnality. A "both/and" ethic in any of these places leads to disaster. But think about how often a "both/and" ethic is wrecked by a false "either/or." The Scripture teaches both grace and obedience, both mystery and clarity, both Jesus' humanity and Jesus' deity, both local discipleship and global missions. To choose one in opposition to the other leads to a false choice that winds up tearing down the whole conversation.

I am glad that you see the Christian imperative to care for orphans and widows. I'm glad

Family isn't simply an incidental matter of biology.

you see it through the grid of the gospel of Christ. I've spent the last decade of my life calling for such a vision. What you're suggesting here though doesn't serve the end you think it serves.

Family isn't simply an incidental matter of biology. You're right about that. Family is built on an already-existing pattern, the pattern of the gospel. That's why our adoption in Christ means we ought to care about the adoption of children. The gospel leads us to the mission, and the mission leads us to back to the gospel. That pattern is missional, yes, but the pattern is also incarnational. Both matter.

Adoption, in Scripture, doesn't

form a different type of family. This isn't an altogether unique sort of relationship. Instead, in the gospel, we are adopted "as sons" (Rom 8:15; Gal 4:5). This language of "sons" is really important because God has already trained humanity to recognize the concept of fathers and sons, parents and children, and he has done so through procreation.

At the very beginning of the biblical story, God commands humanity to "be fruitful and multiply" (Gen 1:28). Then God, almost immediately, takes us to the "begats" of the various genealogies. God's favor and God's mercy are seen in the birth

of children, which the Scripture everywhere regards as blessing.

Why? Well, this is because procreation (like marriage) is a picture of the gospel. God's love for us took on flesh, in the person of our Lord Jesus (John 1:14), an Incarnation that causes us to be "begotten" as the children of God (John 1:12; 3:6-7; 1 John 5:1). The love between Jesus and his church is fruitful, and it multiplies. He stands before his Father, with his people, and proclaims, "Here I am and the children God has given to me" (Heb 2:13).

Adoption only makes sense in light of procreation. A child who is adopted is adopted into an already existing concept, that of parents and children. Scripture uses both archetypes, that of adoption and that of procreation.

If we idolize procreation, as though family were merely about bloodlines, we repudiate the gospel that has saved us. But if we turn away from procreation altogether, adoption is no longer adoption "as

> Adoption only makes sense in light of procreation. A child who is adopted is adopted into an already existing concept, that of parents and children.

> Don't see your potential future love for your birthed children as some scarce commodity that you must then take away from your children you might adopt or foster. Love isn't a commodity.

sons." The metaphor then attaches merely to a living arrangement, not to the natural family. Adoption is more, cosmically more, than a living arrangement. The adoption of children makes sense in light of the begetting of children.

Before we can care for orphans, we must ask why there are orphans in the world. The answer includes a variety of reasons, from divorce to poverty to warfare to natural disasters and the list goes on and on. The best thing that can happen for orphans is for children to be welcomed and wanted, to be received as Jesus always receives little children. Before we can love children as orphans, we must love children as children.

The congregation that disciples its own members and cares for those immediately around, but refuses to join with Jesus in reaching the ends of the earth is not a faithful church. Likewise, the congregation that sends missionaries all over but refuses to love its local neighbors is unfaithful. In either case, an "either/or" leads to error. It should be "both/and."

I would counsel you not to permanently incapacitate your procreative capacity. Even apart from Christian disagreements about contraception or family size, we can all agree that the birth of children is pictured by God as blessing not burden (Ps 127:3).

Don't see your potential future love for your birthed children as some scarce commodity that you must then take away from your children you might adopt or foster. Love isn't a commodity, and it isn't parceled out. Love isn't limited, and it isn't a barrier to ministry.

Love "bears all things … endures all things" (1 Cor 13:7). Have babies, and love your babies. Minister to orphans, and pray for God's wisdom in how best you might care for the orphans and widows in your neighborhood and around the world.

Yes, you are right that marriage and family inhibit the freedom one has to do certain things in ministry. The apostle Paul celebrates those who give up family for the sake of ministry, but this, in the apostolic example, entails a giving up of marriage itself (1 Cor 7:1). Once there is marriage, one cannot simply cut apart the conjugal realities for the sake of ministry.

That's why, for instance, Paul warns against those who would toss aside marital sex for ministry's sake (1 Cor 7:5). The decision to have sex with one another, the Bible indicates, was made at the altar. When a couple has sex, then, they are not "depriving" any other ministry of anything. When they refuse for an extended period of time, though,

> It could be that God will show you how to welcome children both by adoption and by the more typical way.

they are "depriving" one another.

It might be that God will not give you children biologically, and instead will spur you all the quicker toward adoption or foster care. It could be that God will show you how to welcome children both by adoption and by the more typical way. And it could be that your love for the children you welcome by birth might be the signal to your church and your neighbors to love children, and thus welcome children who have been orphaned.

It's "both/and," not "either/or." Adopting for life doesn't demand accepting the knife. ба

For Pastors

From Church Pews
to Church Plants
Adoption culture and the world mission

By Jeremy Haskins

L unch time can be a chaotic in our home. Each day, when my wife calls our six kids to the table, it can get crazy. To help with the chaos, our kids have assigned seats. However, one day my wife decided to break the norm and let the youngest, Jonah, assign everyone different seats.

different seats.

Jonah lined everyone up and began seating them by saying, "Okay, I want the boys on this side of the table. Now, I want the girls on that side of the table." Then turning to his brother Isaac, who was adopted from Ethiopia along with him, he said, "Okay, Isaac. Now, I want the 'browns' to sit over here." Everyone in the kitchen burst into laughter.

Apparently, in Jonah's eyes, we have girls, boys and browns in our family. My wife and I made sure to use this as an opportunity to teach our kids how to delight in their differences without segregating the lunch table. While we must point out the wonderful distinctions we have in our family, we must make sure our kids know that they all have the equal standing as Haskins.

This tendency to segregate around the table has always been a problem for the church. We see it all over the churches in the New Testament. As folks enter the church, first-century ushers met them at the door directing traffic, "Jews over here. Gentiles over there. Masters over there with your slaves seated at your feet. Men here. Women there." And yet the Spirit stepped in to speak to the distinctions in the church saying, "There is neither

While the categories are different in our churches, the problem is the same. And yet, the preaching of the gospel cultivates a culture of adoption.

Jew nor Greek, there is neither slave nor free, there is no male and female, for you are all one in Christ Jesus" (Gal 3:28).

And the Spirit's message still has to be applied to the church today. While the categories are different in our churches, the problem is the same. And yet, the preaching of the gospel cultivates a culture of adoption, we will change the way we view seating charts in the church.

Adoption culture: not just tacking it on

I can assure you that all the sermons I heard in the small-town church I grew up in had

When they just tack on the gospel, the ministry is sure to fizzle out eventually.

the gospel in them. My pastors were intentional in this way. If the passage didn't seem to be evangelistic enough, the preacher would make sure to tack on John 3:16 and an invitation at the end.

All of my pastors loved the gospel and wanted people to come to Jesus. Their heart was to make sure they got in the gospel every service. And yet, such a practice often leads to a tack-it-on understanding of the gospel.

Whatever you're going to do, you've got to tack on the gospel.

This is how many people view the ministries we have in our churches. People who truly love the gospel see needs. They start meeting those needs. They then petition the church to make meeting these needs official ministries in the church. To make the ministry legitimate we have to somehow tack the gospel on it. The thought is that if the gospel doesn't fit with the ministry we should not be doing it. The problem too often with this approach to ministry is that when the people who started the ministry fizzle out, so goes the ministry. And when they just tack on the gospel, the ministry is sure to fizzle out eventually.

The most effective way to create and cultivate our ministries in the church is to let them flow

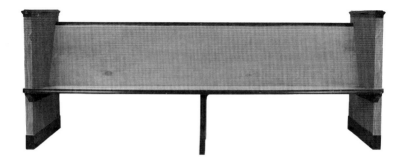

than ministering to orphans and vulnerable children.

This is why at Ashland Avenue Baptist in Lexington, Ky, where I serve as a pastor, we consciously avoid using the phrase "adoption ministry" when we talk about leading and helping families adopt children and care for orphans. Our desire is to cultivate a culture driven by the truth of our adoption in Christ. A culture of adoption when cultivated by the constant and consistent preaching of the gospel not only leads to church unity but to a greater fervency to rescue children from around the world who need adopting.

Understanding who we "really" are

An adoption culture begins with the constant reminder that we are all ex-orphans. What changed everything for us? Adoption! The good news of the gospel is that by God's grace through faith we experienced adoption. In the Son, our status is transformed from poverty stricken orphans to wealthy heirs of God's eternal kingdom. Our churches must cherish this truth of the gospel for us in every home, not just in homes with adopted children.

The danger of creating an adoption ministry apart from this truth is that it only leads to another line in your church's budget. It will become a ministry relegated only to adoptive families and social workers in your church – people personally affected by the orphan crisis on a daily basis. In an adoption culture, everyone has been transformed by the act of adoption and this naturally leads to a desire to rid the world of orphans, both physically and spiritually.

Helping everyone make the connection

The doctrine of adoption in our churches moves us beyond the thought that adoption is only something for infertile couples and families who really love children in need. We have to make the connection for our people

The good news of the gospel is that by God's grace through faith we experienced adoption.

The terms "brother" and "sister" have to be more than cordial greetings. Folks begin to realize that these people really are my brothers in Christ.

between the act of adoption and our existence in the church. The terms "brother" and "sister" have to be more than cordial greetings. Folks begin to realize that these people really are my brothers in Christ. The local church opens up a whole new family for them. This requires that we be intentional and concrete about what the gospel means.

There is much talk today about being gospel-centered. I believe this is good and healthy for the church, as longs as it doesn't keep concepts of grace and mercy in the abstract. Being gospel-centered must also move people beyond an individualistic approach of applying the gospel to seeing how the gospel applies in the context of their own local church.

You must be intentional and specific. People have to be taught how our adoption in Christ changes the way we think about our fellowship with the single mom sitting next to us on Sunday whose rowdy kids continue to distract us in worship. In Christ, she is a fellow heir, not someone who deserves to be seated with her disruptive kids somewhere else.

We must recognize how the family with one kid from Kentucky and another from Kyrgyzstan signals to the cosmos that the gospel transcends bloodlines and makes Christian unity possible. This can only be done through an aggressive intentionality in our preaching that constantly and consistently applies the gospel to the life of the church.

Ex-orphans together for adoption

How does this affect the plight of 145 million orphans and vulnerable children around the world?

To begin with, we need everyone in the church involved in orphan care. We need the 90-year-old woman on a fixed income, who will never adopt. She will never travel to Peru and serve in an orphanage. But you need her connected to

orphan care somehow. When the reality that she is an ex-orphan who has been rescued by the grace of God in Christ becomes real, she will not want to just sit on the sidelines.

Apart from the gospel, the call for every church member to care for orphans makes no sense. By cultivating an adoption culture, through connecting the dots for people, they realize that no matter who, they all have a responsibility to care for orphans physically and spiritually in some way.

In an adoption culture, this reality is constantly pressed upon us. Not just the way we cast a vision for caring for children without families. It's how we understand our mission to reach those apart from the family of God.

A theology of mission

In an adoption culture, the church can develop a clear theology of God's mission in the world. They begin to understand that God is not just generically collecting a faceless group of people out of the world. But, he is determined to form a specific family for himself, the church. Within an adoption culture they realize this family is their family even though it is ultimately made up of people from every tribe, language, nation and

In an adoption culture, this reality is constantly pressed upon us. Not just the way we cast a vision for caring for children without families. It's how we understand our mission to reach those apart from the family of God.

the church. Within an adoption culture they realize this family is their family even though it is ultimately made up of people from every tribe, language, nation and people (Rev 5:9).

In church members' minds, missions means family and central to the creating of this family is adoption. And adoption is something they taste and see in their small groups each week as they live out gospel unity together in their church. They begin to take on a new wisdom. Paul declares, "the manifold wisdom of God is made known to the rulers and authorities in the heavenly places" (Eph 3:10).

Even in the Andes Mountains

In an adoption culture, we point out that this theology of mission, this wisdom, is not to be abstract. Rather, we experience it in our pews each week, as well as the churches we plant around the world.

For example, one of our church planting efforts is in the village of Cordova, Peru, in the Andes Mountains. The driving hope of each child in Cordova is simply to endure each day long enough to get a well paying job in the mines, or head to a nearby city

to further their education. And yet, these children making their way through college or finding a better life outside of Cordova as 'mountain people' is difficult in Peru. The possibility that they end up homeless in one of Peru's major cities is real for each of the children to whom we minister in the village.

During the last five years this void of love and hope has, to some extent, been filled by a group of "gringos" from Lexington. We have witnessed a transformation among the youth of the village just by our presence. Behind their shy looks and whispers to one another, they are overwhelmed with the fact that a group of Americans travel to Cordova to spend time with them.

Ministering to children in Cordova has helped move forward our church-planting efforts. However, we must make sure not to see it as a ploy just to reach the

> It's the whole church realizing we all are needy kids. We all need a loving Father to rescue us and give us a family. We need his care and discipline that teaches us how to love one another and serve those apart from our family.

he called us to make disciples of all nations by "teaching all that [he] commanded [us]."

The day we leave Cordova we must turn to see a church waging war against the Evil One through preaching the gospel, baptizing new followers of Christ and gathering around the Lord's table. And if we are to teach them what these things mean, we will also turn to see them fighting back darkness by defending the fatherless and visiting suffering children in their homes and on their streets.

Conclusion

An adoption culture is much bigger than one segmented group of people who are simply more passionate than everyone else in the church about helping kids in need. It's the whole church realizing we all are needy kids. We all need a loving Father to rescue us and give us a family. We need his care and discipline that teaches us how to love one another and serve those apart from our family. This need can only be met by the power of the Spirit, through the kind of consistent preaching of the gospel that constantly presses its implications upon the church, the adopted family of God. ❧

Orphan Care Ministry

Becoming an adoption-friendly church

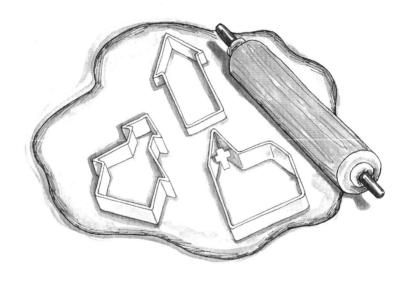

By Kimber Graves

Many churches across the world possess a growing burden for the care of vulnerable children in need of permanent families. Some have been at the forefront of implementing adoption and orphan care ministries within their congregations, while others are still learning what this means and how their own church bodies can offer opportunities for engagement. Church leaders often look to other churches with well established orphan care ministries and feel overwhelmed at the prospect of creating one of their own. But building a pervasive culture of adoption in the local church is not about replicating cookie cutter ministries. Just as each church develops its own distinctive identity in terms of worship and fellowship, churches need to facilitate and support an environment of both adoption and caring for orphans that is uniquely their own.

Undoubtedly, this begins with church leadership, as pastors, staff, elders and deacons set the tone. The congregation will embrace God's heart for the fatherless and the biblical mandate to care for the orphan as leaders communicate this message verbally and through personal life examples. Establishing an adoption culture starts with intentional leaders who offer various opportunities for engagement in the orphan care movement. Consequently, we see a rainbow effect, families sprinkled with children from all ethnicities, from all nations, in our churches.

As churches launch adoption, foster and orphan care ministries in increasing numbers, many families will respond by moving forward to adopt or foster. These

> The congregation will embrace God's heart for the fatherless and the biblical mandate to care for the orphan as leaders communicate this message verbally and through personal life examples.

churches must then choose to make the necessary changes to become adoption-friendly in both word and deed. It is one thing to proclaim a passion for adoption and orphan care; but it is another thing altogether to help make adoption – including preparation and post-adoption care – tangibly feasible.

It is far too common for adoptive families to feel isolated after the adoption is completed,

> More than half of the families even indicated that their pre-adoption counseling did not sufficiently prepare them for their post-adoption experience.

particularly if unexpected issues are complicating a family's home life. Church leaders, vocational and lay, need to ask, "How can we make our church adoption-friendly? What steps can we take to offer the necessary support for adoptive parents and for adoptees alike?"

The adoption un-friendly church

Karyn Purvis, a leading expert specializing in at-risk adopted children, observes that one third of post-institutionalized children transition almost seamlessly into their new families. With some expected adjustments, these children do well without disrupting the day-to-day life of the family. Another third of adopted children bring to their new families moderate concerns which might rock the boat a little, but they do not significantly compromise the integrity of the family. A final third of adopted children will come into the family with such considerable trauma histories that they carry potential for damage to the family unit and it requires a strong, intact marriage and family to maintain stability. Often, outside counsel is necessary to help these children transition into their new families as they begin to heal from the abuse, neglect, and trauma which have left them wounded. These are the situations where marriages are at risk. Siblings are at risk. The very adoptions themselves are at risk.

It is sobering to consider these statistics when viewing a room full of adoptive families. At my church, for example, we have more than 100 adopted children, so it is possible, if not probable, that at least 33 have at some time during their adoption journey experienced substantial struggles, and many of those families are likely suffering in silence.

A 2002 survey conducted by

the Dave Thomas Foundation for Adoption asked married couples where they would turn for information or advice about adoption. Fifty-two percent indicated they would turn to their local church or place of worship. Unfortunately, the post-adoptive statistics are much more grim.

In an effort to learn more about post-adoption experiences, Family Life and Focus on the Family conducted a research study in 2007 called "The Jordan Project," which included detailed responses from more than 400 families. Considering these

families were all constituents of the two ministries, it is safe to assume that many of these were church-going families. The study found that people were nearly twice as likely to turn to their local bookstore as they were to turn to their pastor or church for help dealing with post-adoption issues. Further, though more than half of the respondents reported various post-adoption challenges, only nine percent indicated that they first turned to their church for support in dealing with these issues. Of equal concern, more than half of the families also indicated that their pre-adoption education did not sufficiently prepare them for their post-adoption experience.

Credible adoption agencies should be in contact with these families to provide post-placement support and services, but we also have a role as a church in ministering to the very families we have encouraged to open their homes to vulnerable children. We must decide as a church whether we will simply declare the biblical mandate to care for the fatherless or if we are going to make it safe enough for our families to turn to us – to the local church – rather than the local bookstore – when the faith walk of adoption becomes difficult.

No cookie cutter for adoption culture

Each local church will distinctively serve its families based upon their own unique circumstances and specific needs. Certainly, there is no "one-size-fits-all" type of model to apply toward adoption ministry. One overarching theme, however, which should be foundational to all church families embracing adoption ministry is the acknowledgement of adoption as a lifelong process and the subsequent commitment by the church to support adoptive families regardless of what may come. How does a church like this look?

We should proactively support our adoptive and foster families by

Adoptive and foster families desperately need our churches to present a realistic yet hopeful picture of adoption.

becoming more than mere cheerleaders for the cause of adoption. It is wonderful to talk about awareness; it is heartening to talk about the miracle of adoption. But we must also more honestly consider the needs, realities, and dynamics of these families as they expand. As orphan care and adoption ministries grow within a church, the need for various support systems also increases because the culture of the church is evolving.

Effectively ministering to adoptive families also requires a willingness to learn and become educated on subjects not previously taught in seminary. Staff and volunteers must become familiar with the realities, such as trauma, grief and loss, which often confront these families and their children. In other words, we must fully invest in understanding what adoptive parents are experiencing and why they might parent entirely differently than typical congregants. We need pastors, youth ministers and children's directors willing to attend conferences, workshops and trainings about adoption and its ensuing concerns, and to learn from adoption professionals in the way seminary students are trained by theologians. We need leaders willing to understand that the child throwing a two-hour fit in the children's department might not be a defiant child but rather, could be a fearful, traumatized child who has never learned that adults are people who will keep her safe and meet her needs. Perhaps her only framework is that adults hurt her.

Consequently, our churches need to be honest about the realities of adoption. "The miracle of adoption" is a common catch phrase among the adoption community. Yet, it is also important to acknowledge that all adoption begins with loss and as a result, can bring with it other unexpected emotions such as grief, fear and anger. We do a disservice to the ministry of adoption if we paint it only as a rosy picture, just as it would be a false illusion if we counseled premarital couples that marriage is all romance and roses. Adoption is no different. It is beautiful. It is transforming. But it is also hard. Adoptive and foster families desperately need our churches to present a realistic yet hopeful picture of adoption.

Finally, our churches need to make a long-standing commitment to adoptive and foster families. As we increasingly focus more attention on the needs of orphans and challenge Christians to consider how God might lead them to respond, we must also commit to strengthening and embracing the families who step out in faith to adopt or foster children. This commitment on the church's part must not end when the child arrives home. For families whose transition falls into the more difficult one third, churches must respond, "If it's really, really hard, we are standing with you." Though many families will not fall into that difficult one third, for those who do, it is imperative that we do everything possible to prevent them from being the parents who turn to a bookstore for support rather than to the church. ॐ

Disrupted Adoptions

A new challenge for the church

By Randy Stinson

Post-adoption issues are where we as church leaders currently have our biggest challenge. The Christian community, rightly, has been pushing for more awareness about adoption as a picture of the gospel, and of the need to see adoption as part of the gospel mission. But now, we're realizing that we need to address a number of post-adoption challenges, namely disrupted adoptions.

A disruption is when a family adopts and, for whatever reason, realizes it can no longer take care of the child. And so the family makes a decision legally to end its parental rights. I've come up with my own two types of disruption: crisis disruption and frivolous disruption.

Crisis disruption

The first type of disruption is what I call a "crisis disruption." These are necessary terminations of parental rights when one or more family members are in imminent danger. Generally, I counsel a family to terminate an adoption for the same kinds of situations in which it would remove a biological child from the home: some sort of physical danger or other persistent violation of rules of the home such as drugs or alcohol. I've heard about adopted children who hold other siblings at knife point or sneak into bedrooms at night or choke other children. These kinds of situations are serious and may ultimately end up in termination for safety and other reasons.

We live in a fallen world and sometimes, an adopted child brings a long list of challenges from his or her past. Because my wife and I have adopted several

> A disruption is when a family adopts and, for whatever reason, realizes it can no longer take care of the child.

times, we counsel adopting families in many different circumstances. Along the way, I've learned a few things about crisis disruptions of which church leaders need to be aware.

FIRST
You should believe adoptive parents when they tell you what's going on in the home, unless they give you a reason to think they're incredibly deceptive. We have seen that many times problem children can be manipulative. They might be incredibly difficult at home but incredibly sweet in public. These families end up feeling isolated because no one recognizes the problems they face. You want to make sure you don't isolate families with a crisis adoption.

SECOND

Churches must help families going through crisis disruptions. Many larger churches have ministries that help provide resources for adoption and orphan care. But in most churches, only one or two families adopt at a given time. In these cases, it's incumbent on a church to come alongside the family and help them network and gather resources.

THIRD

Parents sometimes simply do not attach to the adopted child. The exact reasons and explanations aren't for me to determine, but in the end, churches need to say to the adoptive parents, "You can't do this anymore. You can't treat this child differently from the other children. You can't neglect them in this way." Each church's leadership needs to determine when and how they engage these situations. And, in some cases, it may be a church discipline issue.

Frivolous disruption

The second type of adoption disruption is what I call "frivolous disruption." These happen not because of danger, but disillusionment. There's no danger involved for the adopting family, but somehow the adoption didn't turn out the way the parents

> Churches need to say to the adoptive parents, "You can't do this anymore. You can't treat this child differently from the other children."

thought it would.

For church leaders, I offer a handful of reasons why or how families become disillusioned.

Wrong motives

Families become disillusioned when they adopt for the wrong motives. Here are some examples of wrong motives in adoption:

GUILT

Sometimes, when a family finds that a relative is giving up a child, it feels obligated to adopt in order to preserve its bloodline. Out of sheer guilt, the couple says, "We have to do it." That's not a good motive. Or maybe, a couple adopts from a general sense of guilt over its affluence. You don't want people in your church to think that the only way they can prove their care for widows and orphans is to adopt an orphan. It's the wrong motive.

THE ROMANTIC IDEA OF ADOPTION

Adoption is a feel-good act. During the adoption process, people slap you on the back and tell you what a great person you are. People can be swept up into the idea of adoption. And then a child comes into the home, and people stop slapping you on the back and now you have to raise the child. We have to be aware that couples sometimes adopt simply because they love the idea of adoption.

SALVATION-ADOPTION

Couples often think that a child will fix their lives. They've got all sorts of problems, but if they adopt, they think either God will bless them in some kind of immediate way, or their family will rally around the adoption and thereby fix certain problems. But children typically don't fix a problem. They create problems. Ultimately children bring joy, but there can be thorns on the rosebush along the way.

MARRIAGE-BUILDER ADOPTION

This is one of the most common reasons people adopt. A husband and wife aren't doing well. The husband is distant and unengaged. But when the couple talks about  adoption, all of sudden they're unified about something. The two think that an adoption will fix their marriage. So they go through the process and it does feel like the marriage is better because they're talking more and they're excited about something. Then the child comes. And things go back to the way they were before. Children should be the product of strong, healthy marriages. They don't fix marriages.

Wrong expectations
A HALLMARK EXPERIENCE

Sometimes a family will adopt a child and it doesn't experience the

> As leaders, we need to press in on them, not in an intrusive way, but in a loving, caring way to say, "We know there could be some challenges; tell us what they are, we'll help you walk through them."

Hallmark moment. They thought that rainbows were going to come out; birds were going to be chirping. It's a false expectation.

A QUICK TRANSITION

When a husband and wife get married, it takes some time to make the adjustment to living under the same roof. Adoption is similar. Couples shouldn't expect a quick transition. It may take a while. It may take a year, maybe two. Don't expect some kind of immediate, smooth transition. The older the child, the longer it may take.

IMMEDIATE GRATITUDE

Just because you've rescued a child, don't expect him or her to know it or appreciate it immediately. Having a new pair of Nikes and their own bedroom is not going to immediately overcome the challenges of a new place absent from everything they have known. They will often yearn for the place from which they came. Frivolous disruptions occur when parents are personally offended at this very natural reaction.

A two-pronged solution

I propose a two-pronged approach to help pastors and church leaders with disrupted adoptions: pre-adoption counseling and post-adoption care.

PRE-ADOPTION COUNSELING

Pre-adoption counseling is about asking good questions. Probably the most important questions to ask potential adoptive parents are, "Why are you adopting?" and "How is your marriage?" There needs to be unity in general. A problem is that a lot of men don't want to adopt. Many times, the wife wants to do it, but the husband isn't sure. The church can help to make sure that both the husband and the wife are both committed.

Couples need to ask questions like: "Do we have enough financial margin in our life?" "Do we think we can handle more kids?" "What are our life expectations?" These are questions that the church can come alongside and help families considering adoption think through. Church leaders put steps into place before a couple gets married in their congregations. We ought to put something similar into place for adoptive parents.

POST-ADOPTION CARE

Post-adoption care is about intentionality. In many churches, when a couple gets married, there's a newlywed class for them. We ought to offer

something similar to families growing through adoption. Sometimes parents going through a crisis may feel embarrassed by it. That's why church leadership must be proactive and come alongside these families. I know a family who has adopted several children and then they adopted another child and this one challenges them in a way they've never dealt with before. Now the couple is embarrassed because they think they should be able to handle adoptive issues. As leaders, we need to press in on them, not in an intrusive way, but in a loving, caring way to say, "We know there could be some challenges; tell us what they are, we'll help you walk through them."

Conclusion

Adoption and its centrality to the gospel has made it a growing movement in the church. Just like other movements, the church not only needs to pursue it, but make sure it is examining the movement to ensure it is rightly positioned to offer correctives and solutions for problems that will naturally occur. May God be pleased to strengthen the families who have embarked on the incredible adventure of adoption, and may he use the church and its leaders to do so. ❧

Orphan Care Isn't Charity

Spiritual warfare in adoption and orphan care

By Russell D. Moore

We evangelicals often seem to identify more around corporate brands and political parties than with each other in our local churches. But our adoption in Christ makes us not warring partisans but loving siblings, whom the Spirit has taken from the babble of Babel to the oneness of Pentecost. The church's unity attests to the "manifold wisdom of God" (Eph 3:10). Would our gospel be more credible if "church family" wasn't just a slogan, if "brothers and sisters" was more than metaphor? What would happen if the world saw fewer "white churches" and "black churches," fewer "blue-collar churches" and "white-collar churches," and fewer baby boomer and emerging churches, and saw more churches whose members have little in common except the gospel?

Our churches ought to show the families therein how love and belonging transcend categories of the flesh. Instead, though, it seems God uses families who adopt to teach the church. In fact, perhaps we so often wonder whether adopted children can really be brothers and sisters because we so rarely see it displayed in our pews. Some – maybe even you – might wonder how an African American family could love a white Ukrainian baby, how a Haitian teenager could call Swedish parents Mom and Dad. The adoption movement is challenging the impoverished hegemony of our carnal sameness, as more and more families in the church are starting to show fellow believers the meaning of unity in diversity.

That's why adoption and orphan care can ultimately make the church a counterculture. The demonic rulers of the age

Our enemies would prefer that we find our identity and inheritance in what we can see and verify as ours – the flesh – rather than according to the veiled rhythms of the Spirit.

hate orphans because they hate babies – and have from Pharaoh to Molech to Herod to the divorce culture to malaria to HIV/AIDS. They hate foster care and orphan advocacy because these actions are icons of the gospel's eternal reality. Our enemies would prefer that we find our identity and inheritance in what we can see and verify as ours – the flesh – rather than according to the veiled rhythms of the Spirit. Orphan care isn't charity; it's spiritual warfare.

A new household economy

After we learn more about our gospel identity, we start reflecting the economy and priorities of our new household. The God of Israel consistently urges his people to care for the orphan, the widow and the immigrant (Deut 24:17-22) by noting his adopting purposes as "Father of the fatherless" (Ps 68:5). He announces, "If you do mistreat them, and they cry out to me, I will surely hear their cry" (Exod 22:23). The Spirit drives us not just to cry "Abba" in the Christian gospel, but also to respond to the cries of the weak through Christian mission.

Orphan care is, by definition, missional. Paul's letter to the Romans, which includes perhaps the clearest explanation of the doctrine of adoption, isn't a systematic theology text; it's a missionary manifesto, calling the church in Rome to unify and to join Paul in making Christ known to the nations (Rom 15:1-21). This is why James – the brother of Jesus – tells us that caring for widows and orphans is the essence of "pure and undefiled" religion (1:27). And Jesus himself – adopted by the righteous Joseph – identifies himself with the "least of these my brothers" (Matt 25:40).

And he tells us that the first time we hear his voice in person, he will be asking if we did the same.

Imagine, for a moment, the plight of an orphan somewhere out there. With every passing year, she will become less "cute," thus less adoptable. In a few years, on her 18th birthday, she will be expelled from the system. She might join  the military or find job training. Maybe she'll stare at a tile on the ceiling above her as her body is violated – alone or before a camera crew of strangers – by a man who's willing to pay enough for her to eat for one day. Maybe she'll place a revolver in her mouth or tie a rope around her neck, knowing no one will notice except the ones who have to clean up afterward. This story could just as well describe a boy who is orphaned. Can you feel the desperation of what it means to be an orphan? Jesus can. Orphans are his little sisters and brothers. He hears them.

In saying that orphan care is missional, I do not mean that every Christian is called to

adopt or foster a child. But every Christian is called to care for orphans. As with every aspect of Christ's mission, a diversity of gifts abounds. Some have room at their table and in their hearts for another stocking on the mantle by this coming Christmas. Others are gifted financially to help families who would like to adopt but cannot figure out how to make ends meet. Others can babysit while families with children make their court dates and complete home-study papers. Still others can lead mission trips to rock and hug and sing to orphans who may never be adopted. Pastors can simply ask whether anyone in their congregation might be called to adopt or foster parent, or to empower someone who is. And all of us can pray – specifically and urgently – for orphans the world over.

Some would seek to contrast orphan care – and other so-called social ministries – with evangelism, perhaps even with the gospel itself. But such a dichotomy just does not stand up to biblical revelation. Genuine faith works through love, the Bible tells us (Gal 5:6). The mission of Christ points us, as theologian Carl F.H. Henry reminded the last generation of evangelicals, to a God of both justice and justification.

Since genuine faith is always orphan-protecting, a culture of adoption and evangelism can work together. Indeed, they grow from the same root. Churches that are other-directed instead of self-obsessed in adopting unwanted children will be other-directed instead of self-obsessed in

A conscience that's burdened for orphans, rather than seared over in the quest for more stuff, will be burdened for spiritual orphans.

A church that learns to love beyond the borders of biology will learn to do mission outside the borders of geography.

verbally witnessing to unwanted people. A conscience that's burdened for orphans, rather than seared over in the quest for more stuff, will be burdened for spiritual orphans. A church that learns to love beyond the borders of biology will learn to do mission outside the borders of geography.

A kingdom of rescued children

As the Spirit draws more Christians to orphan care, we also must insist that adoption is not just a backdoor route to child evangelism. Of course, Christians who adopt will teach their children that what they believe is true and ultimately meaningful. Every parent does that and, to some degree, cannot do otherwise. A

secular progressive parent would (rightly) correct racial bigotry or misogyny in his or her child. We wouldn't accuse that parent of having a child in order to export Western democratic values. In the same way, Christian parents will teach their child the message of Jesus, regardless of how the child arrived in their home.

But this doesn't mean that adoption is simply a means to evangelism, any more than biologically bearing children is reproductive evangelism. As those who have experienced gospel adoption, we know it is good for all children to have parents, even parents who do not yet know Christ. We advocate, then, for all orphans and rejoice when unbelievers adopt too, just as we encourage marriage between unbelievers, since marriage witnesses to the Christ-church union even when the married couple doesn't see it. The gospel is better understood in a culture that understands the one-flesh union. Likewise, the fatherhood of God is better understood in a culture where children know what it means to say "Daddy" and "Mommy."

Scripture characterizes the kingdom of Christ as a kingdom of rescued children. Solomon looks to the final reign of God's anointed and sings, "For he delivers the needy when he calls, the poor and him who has no helper. He has pity on the weak and the needy, and saves the lives of the needy. From oppression and violence he redeems their life, and precious is their blood in his sight" (Ps 72:12-14). When we contend for orphans – born and unborn – we do more than cultural activism. A culture of adoption, orphan care, and ministry to mothers in distress announces what the kingdom of God looks like and to whom it belongs. We're contending for the faith once for all delivered to the saints (Jude 3).

While I wrote this article, my children came running through my study hyped up on Kool-Aid and Pop-Tarts (don't judge me). I heard myself saying, "Will all of you please be quiet so I can think?" But I remembered when our house was quiet, and I remembered the silence of the orphanage where we found Timothy and Benjamin. The kingdom of God isn't quiet.

Instead it's like my house these days, "like a flock in its pasture, a noisy multitude of men" (Mic 2:12). The universe around us is creepily silent – like an orphanage in which the children no longer believe they will be heard. But if we listen with Galilean ears, we can hear the quiet desperation of thumbs being sucked, of cribs being rocked. As we welcome orphans into our homes, we can show the orphaned universe what it means to belong to a God who welcomes the fatherless.

Let's remember that we were orphans once, and that someone came looking for us, someone who taught us to call him "Abba." Let's be ambassadors for the One who loves the little children, all the children of the world. Like him, let's welcome children into our homes, our churches and our lives, especially those we are not supposed to want. ✎

Resources

Adopted for Life: The Priority of Adoption for Christian Families and Churches (Crossway 2009), Russell D. Moore

Moore to the Point
The online home of Russell D. Moore, the Moore to the Point blog contains dozens of posts and articles about and related to adoption. For access, visit www.russellmoore.com and search "adoption."

Bethany Christian Services
Bethany Christian Services is a global nonprofit organization caring for orphans and vulnerable children on five continents. Bethany is recognized as a prominent leader in social services worldwide, and is the largest adoption agency in the U.S. Founded in 1944, their mission calls us to demonstrate the love and compassion of Jesus Christ by protecting and enhancing the lives of children and families around the world. www.bethany.org

Christian Alliance for Orphans
The Christian Alliance for Orphans unites more than 100 respected Christian organizations and a national network of churches. Working together, its joint initiatives inspire, equip and connect Christians to "defend the fatherless" (Isa 1:17). www.christianalliancefororphans.com

Together for Adoption
Together for Adoption exists to provide gospel-centered resources that magnify the adopting grace of God the Father in Christ Jesus and mobilize the church for global orphan care.
www.togetherforadoption.org

From Southern Seminary

Also in the Guide Book Series from SBTS Press:

A Guide to Biblical Manhood
(SBTS Press, 2011 $5.99),
Randy Stinson and Dan Dumas

PUBLICATIONS FROM SOUTHERN SEMINARY

Southern Seminary Magazine
Towers: A News Publication of The Southern Baptist Theological Seminary
The Southern Baptist Journal of Theology
The Journal of Discipleship and Family Ministry
The Southern Baptist Journal of Missions and Evangelism

CONNECT WITH SOUTHERN SEMINARY ONLINE

News.sbts.edu
Facebook.com/SBTS
Twitter.com/SBTS

For more information about Southern Seminary, visit sbts.edu; for information about Boyce College, visit boycecollege.com

Contributors

Editor

RUSSELL D. MOORE is dean of the School of Theology and senior vice president for academic administration at The Southern Baptist Theological Seminary. Moore is the author of several books, including *The Kingdom of Christ*, *Adopted for Life* and *Tempted and Tried*. Moore is married to Maria and they have five children, two of whom were adopted from Russia.

Contributors

DAN DUMAS is senior vice president for institutional administration at Southern Seminary, and a pastor-teacher at Eastside Community Church in Louisville, Ky. He is the husband of Jane and the father of two adopted sons, Aidan and Elijah. Besides being a devoted follower of Jesus, he is passionate about being a transformational ministry architect, teaching the next generation of pastors and leaders and creating gospel-saturated events and conferences. In the little margin left he loves all things sports, especially water sports and enjoys being an avid outdoorsman.

KIMBER GRAVES is an adoption specialist for Bethany Christian Services, where she has worked for eight years, serving children and families throughout the state of Indiana. She is also the post-adoption coordinator at her church, Highview Baptist, in Louisville, Ky. A graduate of Hendrix College in Conway, Ark., Graves previously worked for James Dobson at Focus on the Family. Graves is committed to assisting parents as they prepare for the lifelong process of adoption and empowering them with the tools to help children heal while maintaining healthy families. She lives in Sellersburg, Ind., with her husband and three children, two of whom were adopted from China.

DAVID "GUNNER" GUNDERSEN is a doctor of philosophy candidate in biblical theology at Southern Seminary and serves as director of student life at Boyce College. He and his wife, Cindi, have four children, all adopted from East Africa: Judah, Ember, Isaiah and Brooklyn. Gunner enjoys family, sports, words and fall weather.

JEREMY HASKINS is pastor of the mission at Ashland Avenue Baptist Church in Lexington, Ky. Ashland Avenue seeks to be a model church when it comes to orphan care and adoption. Jeremy has been married to Danae since 1998. God has blessed them with six children. They have four boys and two girls. In July of 2009, God blessed them with two boys through adoption from Ethiopia. Jeremy graduated with a master of divinity from Southern Seminary in 2008.

TIMOTHY PAUL JONES serves as associate professor of leadership and church ministries at Southern Seminary. He is the author or coauthor of more than a dozen books. *Christian Retailing Magazine* awarded Jones top honors in 2010 for his book *Christian History Made Easy*. Jones earned the bachelor of arts degree in biblical studies and a master of divinity with focus in biblical studies and historical theology, as well as the doctor of philosophy degree from SBTS. He is married to Rayann and they have adopted two children, Hannah and Skylar.

RANDY STINSON is the dean of the School of Church Ministries at Southern Seminary. He has been married to Danna for more than 20 years. They are the parents of seven children: Gunner, Georgia, Fisher, Eden, Payton, Spencer and Willa, four of whom they adopted. He teaches a young couples Bible study at Highview Baptist Church in Louisville, Ky.

Production

MANAGING EDITOR:
AARON CLINE HANBURY, whose career began with the *Tampa Tribune,* is a journalist from Jacksonville, Fla. The son of an adopted father, Aaron is the managing editor of Southern Seminary's "Towers" news magazine and assistant editor of *Southern Seminary Magazine.* He lives in the Crescent Hill neighborhood of Louisville, Ky.

DESIGNER:
ANDREA STEMBER joined Southern Seminary's creative team in 2011 after working four years in the Chicago, Ill., graphic design scene. Though she loves the city, Andrea was born and raised in the state of Iowa, where she earned her bachelor of fine arts degree in graphic design from Iowa State University. She has been married to Daniel for two years.

ILLUSTRATOR:
ROBIN TILLMAN has been married to Robert for 26 years and they are the parents of five children, one of whom they adopted from China in 2004. Robin is an artist and art teacher. She currently works as a freelance artist and teacher in a variety of settings in Louisville, Ky.